Church Hurt, then Church Healed

When Focusing on the Messenger, Distracts You from the Message.

By ALEXIS MILLER

Live in the present, and Don't Deny Your Past
-MAYA ANGELOU

"If you can't figure out your purpose, figure out your passion. For your passion will lead you right into your purpose."
-Bishop TD Jakes

Endorsement

"Alexis Miller, has tapped into a subject that is so timely for the body of Christ right now. Many people leave ministries wounded, and never have made it back, all because their faith was in their Pastors or leaders to be perfect. Alexis reveals that it's possible to be church hurt, but it's also possible to be church healed."

"I am grateful for Alexis' boldness to share her story, to encourage and empower others."

-Pastor Sheila L. Ashley
Total Agape Ministries
Warner Robins, GA & Atlanta, GA

Dedication

This memoir is dedicated to my three Princes, Jaden, Keon, and Deon. Mommy loves you all with everything in me. I want you to know that you can do anything through Christ, who strengthens us. Thank you, boys, for loving mommy in spite of.

To My Parents, thank you for loving me and allowing me to go after my dreams. Daddy you are so special to me, and Mommy your faith is what have inspired me to continue. I love you Darrol and Victoria Singleton.

To all past and present members of SANE Church Int'l, now El Elyon Ministries, I love you and you will always be my family. It is indeed Recovery Season.

Table of Contents

Introduction

The first time God placed it in my spirit to write this memoir, I knew I had to do it without shame. I had no idea why he chose me and why he would want me to be so transparent about my skeletons but I knew he had a purpose. Although, the thought of it made me nervous, I knew that if my story could help just one person than God's will would be done. I had no specific instruction on when and how to start but as soon as I accepted it in my heart, God would slowly drop things in my spirit.

This was two years ago and I was just able to finish this book at the beginning of 2016. We never know how long it takes to do the things God has asked, we just have to accept it and continue. I had no idea I would endure so much more strife in the process. I stand with you today and say that, when you walk into your purpose you will be enamored at God's mysteries. Many distractions and obstacles may have come along the way but with God's divine guidance and will, the task was finally completed. I wrote this memoir with my whole heart and passion for our younger generation. The times that we are in is very critical.

We all need our own personal relationships with God more than ever before. It is time for us to be true to ourselves and to put an end to childish ways. Once we come into knowing how much our father loves us, we should start to pay attention and seek his will.

Since the day I have rededicated my life to the Lord, it has been a fight, but it's a good fight, a fight meant to win. Not every day is rough and not every day will be easy.

I have learned even through the rough days, the days I feel discouraged, the days I don't feel like continuing that I should still praise him and push through. Sometimes all it takes is an utterance and he will hear us.

Honestly, I must say to you I have had moments that I was just like wow! Why is it so hard to live righteous? The enemy wants us to think his way is easier. Seriously, I know this to be true for myself, I understand what you may go through because we are all human.

The facts in it all is that, it may seem that the opposing side is easier. But the whole time it is a big fat lie, he tells us false tales. Personally, I can say I tried a lot of his tricks. I fell for the lies for a while, somehow I always would still feel empty. The temporary comforts would only work for a short period of time before reality would kick right back in. That is the part that is set up to drain us, emotionally, spiritually, and physically.

At 32 years old, I can honestly say I have a peace in my spirit and agape love for all of my brothers and sisters in Christ. I feel you, we are in this together and just know that we can make it.

Let's just continue to encourage one another. Try building someone up, as oppose to tearing one another down. After reading my story, I would hope that you read with the understanding that we will never be perfect. We may have our personal struggles and battles to fight, but we can win. The difference is this time, we repent when we fall, and try harder next time not to make the same mistakes. "When you know better you do better." (Maya Angelou)

Chapter 1

A Child of Faith

How many of us aren't supposed to be here—or were told that we weren't?

Exactly. A lot of us have heard our parents tell the strange stories and scenarios that led up to our conception and birth. Here's mine. My mother had two sons before me and didn't plan to have another. In fact, she was planning her divorce and her escape from her bad marriage to our father—who, I should mention, was once a handsome and intelligent man, before he suffered from the spirit of drug addiction. My mother loved him dearly, but she couldn't keep suffering his verbal and physical abuse. Just as she was on her way out of her marriage, God surprised her with the news of her pregnancy.

My mother wasn't happy at all. She was devastated. Her plan was to move on with her two boys, to leave her broken marriage and rebuild her life as a divorced woman. But God had other plans, and I made it to this world. I thank the Lord for my very strong grandmother, who was deeply rooted in prayer. My grandmother prayed for me to make it and for my mom to have a healthy pregnancy.

God sent me to my mother because shortly after I was born, she was to lose her father, who was also her best friend. God knew she would not be able to handle it all alone at that season in her life, so he blessed her with my godparents. Robert and Shirley Dupre were truly angels sent to help my mother care for me when I was a new baby in the world. I never went without necessities, and they loved me as if I were their own daughter. They have always been a huge part of my life, especially in my childhood and my teenage years.

From the beginning, God is with us. He creates us already knowing his purpose for our lives. No matter how our lives start or what twists and turns they pass through, God's purpose and testimony are always revealed at one point or another. The measures that were taken to prevent me from being here failed because the Word is simple. I was created a child of faith from the start. On May 26, 1984, I was born, and God had a purpose for my life, just as he does for all of you.

Ever since I was a kid I've been outspoken and outgoing. I was never shy around family or friends. Throughout Head Start, elementary school, and high school, I never had a problem making friends or talking to people. It was in elementary school that I first discovered my love for poetry and acting. If there's one thing I was made for, that I enjoy and would happily do for free, it's reciting dramatic monologues. God blessed me with teachers and family members who cultivated this in me. They gave me the knowledge I needed to succeed in my craft.

My mother moved from Eunice to Sunset, a very small town in Louisiana where everyone knows everyone else. In sixth grade, she joined the Zion Travelers Baptist Church. It may not have been many members, but she made sure we were there at least two Sundays a month to worship God and hear his words. My grandfather was a deacon, and he lead intercessory prayer every Sunday. His voice and call to God were like music to my soul, and it was at that time that I learned how to pray. Every Sunday, he showed me through his prayers how to call on the Lord. My grandfather couldn't have realized how big an impact he was making on my spiritual life or how much was pouring into my spirit. But I thank God for the late Francis Singleton, Sr.

My Aunt Willie was my sixth-grade teacher, and conveniently my school was directly across the street from our church. It's almost like God positioned her class to point in the direction of the church doors.

My aunt wrote a school play for us, and I played the leading role. That was my first acting part: I was a "praying grandmother."

The part was inspired by my mom's mom, my own grandmother. I remember praising God and catching the Holy Ghost in the play. It was normal for me to do so, because I had been raised around church women. The praise felt completely familiar to my soul, and I'll never forget that moment. Everyone enjoyed the play, too, and God's plan to display my talent was carried out that day. Afterwards, it grew like ripples on a pond. I had teachers asking me to recite poems and give dramatic interpretations, both for school programs and in contests outside school.

A few teachers took special time to teach me acting and public speaking skills. One of them, by the name of Betty Mitchell, was the sternest teacher you could ever meet. Everyone feared her discipline and her no-nonsense attitude. I could laugh thinking of how we'd get into trouble and she'd paddle us for it. Well, Ms. Mitchell saw something in me that stood out to her, and she took great care teaching me to recite poems like "Phenomenal Woman" and "Still I Rise" by Maya Angelou. She taught me proper pronunciation to help my audience understand me. She showed me how important delivery was for the monologues. She always reminded me that speaking is more effective when your audience can feel your words, not just hear them. She spent many hours every week guiding me and training me, and her hard work paid off. I was soon awarded in contests all over Louisiana for my work. I went on to compete in many different cities and for different organizations, and I always placed first.

I thank God for my Aunt Willie and for Ms. Mitchell. God chose them to teach me to use my gifts and to sow the seeds of success in my heart.

From sixth to eighth grade, I was known throughout southwest Louisiana as a talented and outgoing young lady. At the end of eighth grade, another special woman in my life, Ms. Cheryl, told my mom and me about an upcoming pageant she thought I should enter. This was Hal Jackson's Talented Teen Pageant. I had never heard of it, but we did our research and discovered that it was a big deal all over the US. My talent would be displayed through a three-page long dramatic interpretation of two characters. The interpretation would be a Prayer between a woman and God. The woman is outraged and hurt that God made her black. She goes on to ask him why and then, God answers her. I loved it from the first time I read the dramatic interpretation.

Mark 11:22
And Jesus answering saith unto them, Have faith in God.

Chapter 2

Gifts and Talents

That year, the poem that changed my life was placed in my hands by my Aunt Willie. My teachers and family had decided together that if I were to enter this talent-driven pageant, I should learn and deliver the dramatic interpretation "Why Did You Make Me Black," by Runell Ni Ebo. I had never heard of Runell. Google had just been founded back then, and the internet wasn't a household thing yet, so I didn't learn much more of her. All I knew was that she was talented, and the words she wrote in that poem came alive for the next year of my life.

My teachers and my aunt coached me through the poem until I could eat, sleep, and recite it. "Why Did You Make Me Black" is a powerful monologue, and I grew more excited and passionate every time I went over it. In May of 1998, after months of training, I finally had pageant rehearsal, and I was ready for it. It was very intimidating. I was competing with talented singers and ballet and tap dancers. I was also the youngest person there. I was barely 14 years old, and I had just finished eighth grade. But I was confident that my talent would override my age.

They rehearsed with us and prepared us for the pageant. They told us its history and all about Hal Jackson's extraordinary career. He was a black radio pioneer who founded the WBLS station in New York and paved the way for black radio stations all over the United States. He was a gifted and talented man who was highly respected. His daughter, Jane Harley, helped him organize the Talented Teen Pageant to highlight young women from every state and a few islands. Each state or island's winner would go on to compete in the International Pageant, which was to be held in Harlem, New York, that year. The pageant had been going on for thirty years when I entered, and many celebrities had been a part of it, including the actress Sheryl Lee Ralph, the late Michelle Thomas from Family Matters, and many others. I was deeply thankful that Mrs. Monroe had asked me to enter it.

On the day of the pageant, it seemed like nothing went right. My hair was not done, I couldn't get a last-minute appointment for it, and my dress was having malfunctions. At one point during the day, I wanted to just pull out of the pageant because it seemed like everything was going against me. But my best friends and my mom encouraged me not to give in, and to just go with what I had. My 15-year-old cousin and best friend Brittany had a passion for doing hair, and she practiced by styling mine. So we let her do my hair that day. She did her best, and I am forever grateful that she did. My brother's girlfriend let me borrow her prom dress. We pulled everything together, and I made it to the pageant venue. The other girls looked at me like I was crazy. They thought I was too young to be competing with them in the pageant. I was only 14, and they were all 16 or 17.

There were many obstacles facing me that day, and the whole experience would have ended if I had given up over the things that went wrong or didn't go the way we planned. But I'll never forget when my turn came to perform and I went to the back. While I was changing into my performance attire, I prayed silently and asked God to clear my mind so that I could deliver my monologue and that his will be done. Even as a teenager, I was always in touch with my spirit, and I always went to God boldly. I asked God to go out on that stage with me that day and to perform through me. Before I knew it, I was stepping out onto the stage, and it was like the spirit of strength and God's love filled my entire body. I bowed my head before I started to speak, and when I looked up I felt like a new person. Every word came out of my mouth with power, and I still remember how the judges' eyes sparkled with amazement, like they were stunned that such a young girl could recite a poem with so much tenacity and charisma. At the end of my monologue, all three judges rose to their feet and gave me a standing ovation along with the entire audience.

Being the youngest person crowned with the winning title was an honor and a major milestone in my life. I went on to compete in the international pageant that July at the Apollo Theatre in New York City. The Louisiana pageant committee and my mom held many fund-raisers in our state to help us to go. I was in so many newspaper articles that I couldn't keep up. I traveled all around my state. I also did various syndicated radio shows. It was an awesome experience to be honored as Miss Talented Teen Louisiana.

In New York, we were given the royal treatment. I met talented young ladies from all over the United States, and we all greeted each other respectfully in our crowns and sashes. The week was full of extravagant experiences. We had dinner on the Excalibur Yacht as we sailed around the Statue of Liberty. We went to galas and met celebrities who came to speak to us on different panels. Finally, the big pageant day came, and we were all nervous.

I placed third, which made history for Louisiana. No one from my state had ever placed in top ten in the thirty years the pageant had been running. God was showing me the beginning of his smile. At the pageant, I also met many people: producers, talent agents, and script writers for hit shows and movies. They were all very warm and welcoming to me. They gave me their contact information, and asked my mom to stay in touch. In the case that anything came up that I might be interested in. I felt comfortable meeting such important people, and having them think I was talented was a success in itself for me—a little girl from a small town in Louisiana making a splash in the Big Apple.

Three months later, Jane Harley personally invited the Louisiana committee to Los Angeles for several workshops. We raised money, and once again my wonderful mom extended herself so that we could take the trip. This was a special trip I was chosen by

Ms. Harley to attend, because not everyone from the pageant was invited. We traveled to Hollywood, and I experienced another awesome milestone. The workshops were enlightening, and the tools we learned were important. I connected with the producers of the *Moesha* show at one of the workshops, and they'd already seen a video of me from the pageant. They thought I was amazingly talented, and they told my mom they thought I really had a chance in Hollywood. One producer insisted that we consider moving if we were able to. My mom laughed and said, "I have faith in God and in my daughter's talent, but we don't have the means to move to California."

Still, we exchanged information with the agents and producers in hopes that building relationships would help us learn the business. We were able to go to a live taping of *Moesha*, we visited the Walk of Fame, and we attended more acting and industry workshops. It was the most fascinating week of all my childhood memories. I felt like I belonged there in Hollywood, it was so settling to my spirit. Everything felt familiar and normal. I remember walking down the Walk of Fame saying that one day my name would be there.

When we returned to Sunset, nothing was the same. My visions were different, my faith grew stronger, and I felt like I had found a part of the world where I could finally belong and do what I love to do. I knew there was a way to get back there, and I knew that it was part of God's will for my life.

It was through that season that I learned the power of prayer. One day after school in ninth grade, I fell on my knees beside my bed with the door closed with no one listening but God. I prayed a secret and cried out to the Lord. I said, "Lord, I know you did not show me those things in Hollywood without purpose. God, I am trusting you to open the doors so that we can move to Hollywood. I know I need proper training, and I would love to sign an acting contract with a talent agency." I said, "Lord, I know you are real. I have faith that if this is your will for my life, you will open the doors that would allow my family move to California." I promised God that I would be on my best behavior and obey his word.

It was just a few days later that one of the producers from *Moesha* reached out to us, saying that his wife was interested in signing me to her talent agency, "The Coloring Book." He insisted that my mom seriously consider my future in acting and the possibility of moving to California, because great opportunities were presenting themselves to us. My mom's first response was that she had no doubt that her daughter was talented and she had the faith to step out into the world. Her concerns were about finding a place for us to live and how my dad would receive the news of us moving. Two weeks later, my dad said he had faith in me too but he wouldn't move to California. Instead, he said he would stay in Louisiana and maintain our home there until we were situated and my career was off to a good start. My brother was in college at the time, so he would stay in Louisiana too. Shortly afterward, someone called offering to rent us a guest house in Altadena, California. My mom and I prayed together about everything.

Before we knew it, God was making provisions for us to relocate to California.

Altadena: new beginnings, new outlooks, new awakenings. The lady that we rented from was very gracious and rarely around, her name was Adele. My mom and I fit right in. I enrolled in John Muir High School in Pasadena and met many students who welcomed me. I was very careful about who I shared my business with, even why I had moved to California. The only thing most of my peers knew was that I was a country girl from Louisiana who had moved there with my mom. But I made friends with a funny and handsome guy who made me laugh every time we spoke. I did tell him why I had moved to California and what I would do every day after I left school.

One day I invited him to come along with us to the set of *Moesha*. My agent's name was Teri and her husband, T. Smith, was one of the co-producers of the show. T was also one of the people who inspired my mom and I to move. Teri and T became my second family, and I grew very fond of them. Their daughter, Taylor, was adorable, and they both had successful careers in Hollywood. I always felt blessed to be connected with them. There was a taping of the show every week, and we were always invited to be on set. It was cool to spend time around such talented but humble people. Sheryl-Lee Ralph and Brandy were always very warm to me. I was there so much that the cast and crew grew very fond of me.

The day I invited my high school buddy Jackie Long to the set, everyone fell in love with his humor. He made some very cool connections and was invited to return, and he became an extra on the show. He became friends with Ray J. He eventually became a well-known actor with a few hit movies under his belt. I am very proud of my friend's accomplishments. I always knew he would be a success, and that's why I was always attached to his spirit. God showed up in his life from then to now. Over the years, as I took many foolish turns in life, I would often stop to reflect and somehow see him on television and smile. My buddy's success is a constant reminder of how awesome God is and of how he has always been with me. Although my testimony took a different route, and a longer one, I still know that God is the pilot and that his purpose will be revealed.

I enjoyed every moment of my new life. My agent and I grew closer and closer, and I always admired her. Teri actually took me on a trip to visit her dad in Palm Desert one weekend. She'd never told me who her dad was or that he had ever been in the industry, and I never asked that kind of question. But when we arrived at his doorstep and he opened the door with a huge smile, he was already very familiar to me. Teri's dad was Hal Williams, the dad from *227*. I thought that was hilarious, and it tickled me pink. It's funny how it feels that everything I experienced in those two years in California was pre-ordained by God. Just encountering all of God's minor details along the way tells me now that I am special to him. When Mr. Hal opened the door, Teri's daughter Taylor jumped into his arms. Teri pressed her way inside and helped me with my things. I was surrounded by greatness and none of it was a coincidence. I always knew it was God. It felt like he was putting together the pieces of my life's puzzle even back then.

During those two years, I did get sidetracked from my purpose for being in California. Being only 14 and coming from such a small country town, I needed to adjust to so much in such a short time that I was consumed by the fast pace of the world in California. I take full responsibility for not studying for auditions or focusing on the characters I was given. I realize now that if I had focused more and cherished what God was doing in my life at that time, I would already have been successful at my craft. But sometimes we choose the long route, even when God has a better map for us.

We often visited a church in Los Angeles called the Church of the Harvest. The bishop's name was Clarence E. McClendon. He had indeed been anointed by the Lord, and my mom and I really enjoyed his Sundays services. His church was where I heard one of the most important sermons in my life, one that still has not left me. It was the first sermon I remember touching my soul as a young lady: "Transition, Change, and Transformation."

I knew that we were right in the middle of God's divine plan because I was indeed in Transition. I had no idea how long the stages would last, but I can boldly tell you today—18 years after I heard that awesome man of God's sermon—that I am in the Transformation stage. My heart beats hard just knowing how far God has brought me and how God's time is not our time. I could not have known that it would take 18 years for me, but it did, and I am thankful and glad that God covered me from Glory to Glory.

Every week I started a new journey. It was like I heard the word of God but went back to my normal ways and disobeyed the Father's instructions. I started dating different guys and got distracted from what God was telling me and the reason he had made a way for us to be there. Just as he had opened so many doors for me in Hollywood, he slowly started to shut them, the more I shut him out and started to take on a spirit of "I'm here because I am so talented."

Sometimes we forget that it's God, and that time taught me the lesson that whatever he gives, he can also take it away. I did a few commercials, I was an extra on many shows, and I had the pleasure of working with Mary-Kate and Ashley Olsen on a few of their movies. Megan Good and I had a mutual friend back then who was very sweet to me, and because of her I met many other young celebrities. There were many priceless moments in those two years that I will always hold close to my heart. My mom and I met another mother and daughter in Altadena who we grew very close with for our entire time there. Ms. Gracy was a funny woman and always made us laugh. Nyesha was a friend I could hang out and have fun with. She was very special, and she had a relationship with Jesus Christ that was what I loved most about her.

It was on a Sunday afternoon after church that Ms. Gracy was used as a vessel by God and my life changed once again. I will never forget that evening. We all walked out of a restaurant together, and it was the first time I experienced a true prophetic experience. Ms. Gracy stopped, turned around, and said, "Alexis, God wants me to tell you something." My eyes popped open. Here I was, a 15-year-old girl, thinking *Uh, whoa, what is she about to say?* She said, "God told me to tell you," as she put her hand on my back, "that you made him a promise, and he did something for you to show you who he was in your life, but you did not keep your promise." She said, "God said that you will indeed be successful, and one day you will do exactly what he said you would do. His word will not return to him void. You will be known for your gifts and talents all over the world. But right now is not the time because you are not ready."

I started crying. I knew without a doubt what God had shared with her, because she didn't know about my prayer that one day on the side of my bed in Louisiana. Only God did. And I knew I had broken my promise. I knew that everything I had told God I would do I had not done. I was not obeying him at all, and I knew it in my heart. I had taken God's love and my mom's sacrifices and faith for granted.

When we got home, I said, "Mom, maybe it's not meant for me to make it as an actress right now. Maybe God brought us here so he could sow the seeds of success in my heart." She asked, "Why are you giving up?" I explained that I wasn't giving up. I told her that I just couldn't handle Hollywood right now, that it was too much for me. She wanted to wait a little and said that if I didn't land a big role in those two months, she would agree and we could move home until I finished high school. Closer to the time we moved, she asked me why I'd had such a change of heart, and I honestly told her that it was because I had let God down. Within a month, we had moved back to Louisiana.

{Luke 17:6
And the Lord said, if ye had faith as a grain of Mustard seed, ye might say unto this sycamine tree, Be thou plucked up by the root and be thou planted in the sea; and it should obey you}

We returned to the small town I grew up in,

and I went back to my high school, but I had returned a different person. I say this because I'd been exposed to very different things in California. My outlook on life was different in both good and bad ways, and I'd developed some negative habits. I didn't care about anything anymore, and I felt like my dreams had been shattered. I felt like a failure, so I turned my negativity into promiscuity and rebellion. I hardened my heart.

It is strange how we get mad at God or our lives when everything is our own fault, and how we put so many obstacles in our own paths. I had moved back with a lot to talk about, with many experiences and interesting stories to tell. Shortly after I returned home, the singer Aaliyah was killed in a plane crash. This was hard for me because I had just met her at a movie premiere. She was a humble and sweet young lady. My mom and I took pictures with her and I spoke with her briefly.

In my last two years of high school, I was focused on the wrong things, but school was still important to me. I became the Winter

Formal queen, and I graduated with my class in 2002. My plan was to move back to California to attend acting school and reconnect with the industry friends I had made. But an older friend I'd met at the pageant in New York, one who was like a mentor to me, was working at CNN in Atlanta. She encouraged me to visit there before I decided on Houston or Pasadena. Since I was afraid to move back to Cali alone, and Houston was just like Louisiana to me, I visited Atlanta. Once I did, I was sold on it. Atlanta would be my new home. I fell in love with the city and I met a few friends in the two weeks that I visited. I was appalled at the many opportunities that the city had to offer black people. Louisiana was a different beast. It was rare to see black people in executive positions.

Atlanta was really interesting for me. It's like you could learn your way around the city really fast. It was not overwhelming at all to adjust to. I got lost a few times but I managed to find my way around. Everyone was so welcoming, and I was ignited to go back to Louisiana to get all of my things and move back as fast as I could. My friend that I was visiting with showed me the major highways and short cuts around the city so that I could maneuver around without her.

On Sundays, she would attend Antioch Church and I would visit with her. Atlanta was very comfortable for me and it was no way around me moving. I traveled back to Louisiana only to gather my things. Although, it was hard to say goodbye to my best friends that I was raised near. Everyone understood and they were busy with their own lives as well. My mom was happy for me to move, she always knew I loved the city life and she always wanted me to be in a place where it were more opportunities than Louisiana. My dad on the other hand was really sad. He had dreams that I would stay home and attend college at Southern University. I would be lying if I said that I never thought of it because I did. But I was so drawn by the city that I made myself move and prayed he would get over it soon.

Chapter 3

Grown and Gone Wrong

In June of 2002, I moved to Atlanta and stayed with Angela for a month. I found a job and an apartment quickly and started learning my way around the city. I was immediately attracted to the city's night life and culture. At that time, there was an area called the Clubs of Buckhead where all the popular clubs were located. I immediately got sucked into this life and the social settings that surrounded me. I started attracting older guys and living in the fast lane, and I was totally blinded by what the enemy had set before me. I met new girlfriends who were involved with guys living illegal lifestyles. I was in tune with and amazed by their glamorous lives. Most of my friends were

birthday guy invited us to his house to

older than me, and they all had foreign cars,

Chapter 5

Babes In Christ

My schedule changed tremendously. I went from staying out all night, being late for work, fornicating, and cherishing material things more than my own dignity, to obeying God. Bible study every Tuesday, church on Sunday—sometimes I stayed for two services—then 6 a.m. intercessory prayer Monday to Friday before I went to work at 8:30 a.m. I went from plenty of friends to no friends at all, from secular music to gospel music, and from sex to *no sex at all*. Yes, I was celibate for sixteen months during that season and I was only 20 years old. I also went from always needing people around to spending a lot of time alone and in my word with the Lord.

Chapter 3

Grown and Gone Wrong

In June of 2002, I moved to Atlanta and stayed with Angela for a month. I found a job and an apartment quickly and started learning my way around the city. I was immediately attracted to the city's night life and culture. At that time, there was an area called the Clubs of Buckhead where all the popular clubs were located. I immediately got sucked into this life and the social settings that surrounded me. I started attracting older guys and living in the fast lane, and I was totally blinded by what the enemy had set before me. I met new girlfriends who were involved with guys living illegal lifestyles. I was in tune with and amazed by their glamorous lives. Most of my friends were older than me, and they all had foreign cars, expensive jewelry, and big houses. My life began to move fast too in those years. I was partying, drinking, and jet-setting, taking trips from state to state. Any major event, my friends and I were there. Any exclusive party, we had VIP access. We were constantly shopping in designer stores and wearing all the latest fashions. I call those years the blurry years, because we were moving so much I barely remember most of it.

There was a group of guys in Atlanta who were very popular and had a lot of money. Two of my best friends were dating two of them. I was around a lot of money and was on the party scene all the time. Strip clubs, studios, riding in exotic cars. We would have dinner at five-star restaurants and hit four clubs in a night. I was too young to drink, but I would always sip champagne. The years from 2002 to 2004 flashed passed my eyes, and I wasn't focused on anything but worldly goods. I tried to work a few jobs, but I never stayed committed to anything because my older home girls would give me money to just hang out with them and be around. I would have rolls of money in my designer bags and be able to stay out all night partying with them. I started dating men and even had experiences with a few women. I was 19, not accountable for anything or to anyone, and didn't see anything wrong with it.

One day, though, I got tired and decided to get a job at a collection agency. That was my first attempt to become independent and find some kind of integrity within myself. And even though I would still party on the weekends and hang out with my celebrity friends, I managed to hold that job down longer than any other. One night a popular NFL player was having a birthday party at a club called Insomnia. I had a few friends in town from Dallas. One was a Dallas Cowboys cheerleader and the others were well-known models. They begged me to take them to the party, but the strange thing about that night is that I really didn't want to go.

The whole night was a drag for me and I wasn't having fun at all. All the same, I stayed at the club all night, and afterwards the birthday guy invited us to his house to continue the party. A limo took us there, and everyone was still drinking and listening to music. Some of them were playing video games for shots. I fell asleep for an hour on his couch, and then I told my friends that I had to go and get ready for work that morning. By the time I walked into my apartment, it was 7:15 a.m. I showered and went straight to work.

What a day that was, running on no fuel and drained from the world. I arrived at work and met this one particular woman who was always very sweet to me. Rian was humble and spirit-filled and made it clear that she was a Christian to everyone who worked with us. Every week she walked around smiling, passing out flyers, and inviting people to her church. She always put a flyer on my desk, but it wasn't until that morning that I actually heard her and paid attention. The difference was that I was burnt out from the world, and my heart had begun to crave more.

That one day, I was ready to say yes and visit her church. I asked her for a flyer so that I could get the address. She praised God and went at once to her desk to get the flyer.

That was a Monday. Tuesday was Bible study. I managed to get some rest after work that evening and prepared myself to go to her church the next day. I was determined to make it and really hear what God had to say to me. I wasn't foreign to the Word of God at all. As I said, I was born and raised in the Baptist church. But it was like my spirit was being pulled to the house of the Lord on that special Tuesday, and I'll never forget that day.

After work, I grabbed some food and headed to the church, not knowing who the pastor was or what I was walking into. I'd never asked why the pastor's name wasn't on the flyer. Today, this fact tells me that I was just yearning for the Word and that those other things weren't even a factor.

But the enemy stepped in five blocks from the church. I wasn't paying any attention to my gas needle and I didn't notice that I was running low and the gas light was on. I was just trying to get there for the Word. So I ran out of gas while I was on my way there. I steered slowly to the side of the road, and it was like something spoke to me, saying "Don't Quit, Get There!" In my heart, I felt that the enemy did not want me to get to church that day and hear what God had to say to me. I started sweating and crying. It was a hot summer day in the month of July, and Bible study was starting in just 15 minutes. Softly, I said "God, make a way. I need this," and before I could pick up my phone to call Triple A, I looked to my left and saw a Triple A truck in the passing traffic. I flagged it down and the driver put a gallon of gas in my car so that I could make it.

My heart was so full that I got butterflies because I knew there was purpose in all of it. I parked the car at Cheshire Bridge and walked toward the sanctuary smiling from ear to ear and feeling like I had finally made it. I had made it to hear the Word of the God that I needed so much.

Little did I know that the enemy would try to break my spirit one more time before I arrived. There was a deacon standing at the door, a nice man with a bald head and a big smile, and he stopped me to say, "I'm sorry, young lady, but the sanctuary is full." I dropped my head and my eyes and looked at him in disbelief. I turned around and toward my car, my heart filled with discouragement. He said, "Ma'am, where are you going? We have an overflow room around the other side." I said, "I am so sorry! This is my first time here!" He laughed and walked me to the overflow room, straight to the front row where the projectors were. I found a seat and a Bible and sat down. My heart was smiling again, and I let out a huge sigh of relief.

It amazes me that the enemy worked so hard to keep me from getting there. I just knew that I was right where God wanted me and that it was an important day for me to be in the House of the Lord. My spirit had joy and my heart was comforted to be there. I was convinced that the church was awesome because the parking lot was so full that I had to park across the street. It was so many young people walking into the overflow room that it was even more exciting. I was thinking to myself that if other young women and men were in church on a Tuesday for bible study then I was definitely in the right church. It was very nice and the ushers were very neat and they were organized in moving the flow of the congregation into their seats.

Proverbs 8:17
I love them that love me; and those that seek me early shall find me.

Psalm 27:8
When thou saidst, Seek ye my face; my heart said unto thee, Thy face, LORD, will I seek

Matthew 7:7-8
Ask, and it shall be given you; seek, and ye shall find; knock, and it shall be opened unto you

---

Chapter 4

Saved by His Grace

The praise team was powerful, and they were singing an awesome song. The organ player started playing quietly, and the pastor arrived at the altar. I took a double take and looked around the room to see if someone was playing a joke on me.

This pastor was someone I recognized from the hip hop industry, and I couldn't believe that he was there. His name was Dane. He was a platinum-selling rapper who was signed to one of the hottest record labels in the hip-hop community in the 90s. Every artist on that label was successful and super-talented. They had made a huge impact on the hip-hop community and pioneered the industry as it is now. I had heard that Dane was a pastor and had a church somewhere in Atlanta, but I never thought I would actually visit it—I wasn't even interested, really, because I doubted I could take him seriously as a pastor when I knew him already as a rapper. It was a hard concept to grasp. The thought started messing with my mind, and I felt like I had been tricked into going there. I was thinking, *Wow, you have to be kidding me*. Then it dawned on me that maybe that was the reason his name wasn't on the flyer—so that no one would judge him by his past. Anyway, one thing I did know was that I had gone through so much strife and warfare to get there that I might as well stay and listen to what he had to say.

The moment Dane opened his mouth, his demeanor and posture changed, like milk to bones. After the first sentence, I no longer saw the rapper Dane. I saw Pastor Dane Lewis, and It was amazing at how God had transformed him into a new creature in Christ. God was using him for his glory, and it was a real experience for me.

The sermon taught that day was called "Are you a Hearer or a Doer?" I will never forget it because that was when I fell in love with the Word of God because I could understand it, the way Pastor Dane had broke it down for us..

That moment of hearing the Word was a transitional event in my life. I said, "Lord, you are speaking through him but directly to me. I can and will be a Hearer and Doer of the Word." I knew God was real, I knew his power and what he could do, because he had showed me when I was only 14 years old. "So today, Lord, what would you have me do?" I asked. "No matter what it is, I will do it." Then Pastor Dane said, "Are you saved?" and he gave his altar call, and it was like something propelled me out of my seat into the sanctuary. I couldn't delay getting up; it was like my feet lifted me without me even walking to the altar. He prayed for me, and on that wonderful day in July of 2004, I was saved by the blood of Jesus Christ, and my life would never be the same.

After that Bible study, I refocused my life and

heart on God and I never looked back. I found something that made sense to my life. God. What's better than him? Nothing and I hope that is how you feel also. Not only was I enthusiastic about my new journey, I was also humble enough to receive the Word and admit that I needed God. If Jesus could save me like I was taught that he could and turn me around then I was ready for it. It takes commitment and some form of meekness to accept that we need help. I was ready and I opened my heart to learn the Word, I spent quiet time with the Lord. There were times that I would not ask him for anything, I would just thank him and listen to what he had to say to my spirit. Just listening without talking was a good habit that I started. It is so many distractions and so much background noise in our lives at times that we cannot hear what he is trying to say.

Meditating works, meditating on the Word will give you peace like no other. The beginning of my spiritual walk was unforgettable. Pastor Dane Lewis made everything so real for us. The bible stories were broken down in terms that only someone from our era would appreciate. I think that is why we all loved being a part of the ministry and believed in our Pastor so much. I loved the unity within the ministry and we were all family that loved one another. My first fast with the ministry as a new member was incredible. Many breakthroughs happened during that time. I would read my bible and it was as if the Words were coming off the page. The old me was definitely transitioning into a new person. I loved being saved and I knew that I could stay committed to something so real.

Surprisingly, my family and a few friends were not supporting my change like I thought they would. My parents thought that I was in a cult. My friends said I was certainly doing strange things, and my co-workers just started looking at me crazy. It blew my mind that I was finally doing something positive at only 20 years but everyone around still had something negative to say. Certain things were done so that I could completely consume myself with the word. Like for instance, I gave my television away because I would not watch it anymore. I also stop listening to secular music, it was only Christian or Inspirational music playing in my car. No more gossiping on the phone with family or friends and I totally cut a few people off because they were not respecting my mind about my choices.

We were taught that if we listen long enough to gossip and backbiting then we would do the same. At that point I just refused to entertain anything that was not about God. I guess for many of the people that knew me before, they could not adjust to the new me. But I did not complain I just moved along and spent more time alone. I became people free early into my salvation.

Even now I feel the same way. No matter what you are doing in life some people will always have their own opinions. Think about it, I was saved and on fire for God at only 20 years old and they said that I was in a cult. Being talked about is not a new thing for me, it has been going on my entire adult life whether I was doing something positive or negative. So many seeds were planted in my heart during my early years being saved. I gained so much wisdom from the Word of God and our ministry in those 16months that I have went on and used through my so many parts of my journey. I was convinced that I blocked worldly things out and I was tuned in to the Lord for a reason in that season. I had tunnel vision and I was not allowing anyone to detour my path. I was very strong and steadfast in learning and wanting to be better.

Life lessons come at all stages and all ages. An older woman told me one day at my job that year that God told her to tell me to keep going. Remain focused on my instructions because a day would come when everything I was taught about God I would need. Her wise words made me cling even closer. It was an amazing feeling to be in love with Jesus. People use the term lightly nowadays but I can truly say that Jesus was definitely my boyfriend and I was dedicated to him.

My ears would hear things differently. My heart would receive things that people would say in a different manner also. I was starting to realize that the spiritual realm was real. Of course I would have never known that unless I was intuitive enough and reading the word of God enough to receive it. My heart yearned for more wisdom. I wanted to be the best version of me in every way. I learned that I had to remain teachable and to talk less and listen more. My countenance as a young woman changed. I was calm and I understood when trials would come that it was always a lesson or a reason that I needed to pay attention to. I would meet random people in supermarkets that would open up their hearts to me about problems they were dealing with. Sometimes I felt as if they could feel my spirit and that God would place me around them just so that I could pray and encourage them.

My heart was conditioned in a way that when bad things would happen, I would praise God automatically without complaining. I was no longer living in my emotions, I was just keen in my spirit. It did not take long to put away the old things. I wanted the change, so I did what I needed to embrace the change. I opened my heart, listened to the instructions, and prayed without ceasing at times. As adults when we are ready for a change and we are ready for different results we do things that we wouldn't normally do. I decided to finally surrender and give my all to something and that something was God. I dedicated myself to being faithful to showing up to church when the doors opened. I was obeying what I was being taught. I was making myself a better woman and I was slowly seeing results in my life. Blessings were not falling out of the sky but certain things would happen that would confirm to me that I was on the right track and that I was doing the right thing.

I remember going to the gas station to get gas. I am not sure what had happened that day that had me feeling stoic. I had no expression that day I was just trying to stay focused on what I was doing. I was certainly not trying to get distracted in what occurred to throw my day off. So many times the enemy would throw things at me to distract me from what I was doing and to break my spirit that I was used to it at that point. On that particular day I walked into the gas station to pay for my gas and before I can pull out my money a nice heavy set man pulled his electric scooter behind me and said I will pay for your gas today young lady. He said stay faithful, you are doing the right thing you are set a part for a reason, God will get the glory from that. Then he turned his scooter around and rolled outside. I ran outside crying saying thank you so much for paying for my gas and I asked what was his name, he said, "I'm Ben" and he had a big smile on his face and he said its ok you will be ok and left. I wanted to talk more but he was continuing on his journey and left.

I would meet Ben about three more times at different stores in the area on his scooter. Every time I saw him he was smiling with this joy that I cannot describe. His spirit was amazing and I knew without a shadow of a doubt that he was close to the Lord. He always spoke loving, kind words to me. He encouraged me and never knew my name. My heart would get happy when I would see a scooter because I always thought it was him. The last time I had saw him I told him that I was still saved and celibate and that I was so thankful that I had an angel like him around. I told him that he was special and if he ever needed anything he could ask me. That day he said I do need something I need you to follow me to the home that I live in. I followed behind him slowly on his scooter and he pulled up to the Senior Home in our area. We went inside and it was a few of his friends there and they said hey, you must be the daughter he always telling us about. I looked and said no I'm just a friend and they said oh ok. He introduced me to everyone and It made his day that I was there and greeted them all with respect. I stayed about 10 minutes and then I told him to take care and I hugged him, he was smiling like a True Angel and said thank you daughter and thank you again you made my day with a sparkle in his eyes. He said you will be okay Ben promise you that God will take care of you and you will be okay.

  Something was strange about his conversation it was almost like a farewell to my heart and I felt it strongly. A week later I got hired at a stock trading firm in Atlanta. I was so excited because I had been waiting for the call. I went to get gas after the interview and I suddenly thought about Ben. I decided I would get him his favorite orange soda and take it to where he lived to share my good news and to check on him. Once I got there the grounds felt different to me. It wasn't inviting anymore but I walked in anyway. One of the ladies he introduced me to came to the lobby area and told me that Mr. Ben had passed away the day after I left that evening and no one had my number to call me. They sat me down as tears rolled down my eyes and explained that he didn't have any family. He always told them that I was the daughter he never had and that God gave me to him because I gave him joy.

I didn't believe in angels until that day. It was confirmed that Mr. Ben was like my angel. He was sent to encourage me the day I was sad. He was always around in places, and exactly when I needed his kind spirit around. During that season, I did not have anyone to turn to but God. Everyone else was judging my decision to be saved or had a problem with how I was doing it. But he truly made an impact in my life during those months we knew each other. What I would find out that day was that as much of a blessing as he was to me, I was also a blessing to his life. Isn't God good? He can use a stranger, a co-worker, a homeless person, or even someone that we would not expect him to use. He will use whomever he shall to get his word to us here on this earth. Pay attention when you hear his voice, you will know because you will feel it in your heart. It is never a coincidence it is always our Holy Spirit. Sometimes it may be just a whisper and sometimes it's a loud bang.

Matthew 11:15
He that hath ears to hear, let him hear.

James 1:22
22 But be ye doers of the word, and not hearers only, deceiving your own selves.
Matthew 13:13 Therefore speak I to them in parables: because they seeing see not; and hearing they hear not, neither do they understand.

Chapter 5

Babes In Christ

My schedule changed tremendously. I went from staying out all night, being late for work, fornicating, and cherishing material things more than my own dignity, to obeying God. Bible study every Tuesday, church on Sunday—sometimes I stayed for two services—then 6 a.m. intercessory prayer Monday to Friday before I went to work at 8:30 a.m. I went from plenty of friends to no friends at all, from secular music to gospel music, and from sex to *no sex at all*. Yes, I was celibate for sixteen months during that season and I was only 20 years old. I also went from always needing people around to spending a lot of time alone and in my word with the Lord.

I did all this with joy in my heart. I never complained or even murmured about my quick transition. It's like that was just where I wanted and needed to be. I found comfort in the house of the Lord as a young woman and a believer in the Word. I was a babe in Christ on fire for God, wanting everyone to hear the news I had heard. I relished the words of the Lord that Pastor Dane taught.

He was stern and demanded a lot from his congregation. But I understand why he wanted us to be so serious about the Word of the Lord. He taught that if we were radical in the world with the enemy, then we should be radical in the Word with the Lord so that we could help win souls for the kingdom. I understood his teachings, so I followed his doctrine. I also held him in a very high regard personally. He could do no wrong in our eyes.

Besides, we were all young believers—babes in Christ—and most of us were just getting to know God for ourselves as adults. Most of us didn't have personal relationships with Christ until we were introduced to SANE Church International. The vision was to Save a Nation

Endangered. We heard him, we knew he was hearing from God and his anointing was so strong that sometimes all I could do was praise and worship the Lord.

It felt so good to go from one extreme to the other. I literally went from blowing money in clubs and on material things to tithing, sowing seeds, and doing whatever I could to please the Lord. It excited me to pay tithes after the pastor taught us what tithing was and explained to us about sowing seeds. None of us had ever done that before. Pastor Dane and his wife and spiritual leaders would sow huge seeds. They showed us how sowing seeds would always yield a harvest.

I can look back now and say that we held him at a height that man may not be able to reach. Speaking for myself, Pastor Dane seemed like the closest person to God that I would ever know. I take responsibility for losing sight of the fact that he was only the messenger appointed to deliver God's message to me in that season. But I remember thinking that he was perfect, and that was where I went wrong. We admired him as we would God. God is a jealous God, and I am sure he was not pleased with that.

Outsiders told me that I was getting too deep in and that I would crash if I didn't find balance in my spiritual walk. I would respond to people who gave me that advice as if they were speaking a foreign language—they just didn't know how amazing my Pastor was, and I felt they didn't know God. I paid no attention to their logic. I felt that I was doing the right thing and that the fire I had was true worship. At only 20 years old, I was finally living righteously, and I just knew God was happy with us young radical believers.

This one defining moment arrived for me after I came off a fast we were doing. God told me to sow my car to my brother, who had been going through some personal struggles. God put the idea in my heart that my brother was making progress in his life and had earned a blessing. And God will only ask those that he knows will listen and do the things he needs done. So I didn't question it. I drove my car to my brother's apartment, and the seed was sown. Not once did I worry about how I would get to work, because my job was close to my apartment. For an entire week I walked to work, enjoying every moment and getting to know my neighborhood.

One Tuesday morning, there was a light mist in the air and I was walking with a full heart. The other days, I had been smiling and filled with a joyful spirit, believing that God had a plan. But this particular day was a down day for me in the spirit. For six days I had been walking and catching rides home from work. My faith didn't grow weary in my decision, but my spirit felt weaker than the week before.

Sometimes, as Christians, we are on fire in the beginning but when the things don't happen as we think they should, or as we feel they should, we grow weary. That's what I was experiencing. The work day was done, and a wonderful friend of mine had offered to take me to Bible study. Our jobs were close to one another. That evening, when Pastor Dane reached the podium, he said that he wanted to thank God. He explained that God had told him to walk to Bible study that day, and that he was just now arriving. He said, "I don't know who that was for, but God wanted me to walk with you." Tears rolled down my face and chills ran up my spine as I looked to the sky and thanked God for his love. God was confirming that I was in accordance with his will. God loved me so much that he had asked the pastor to walk. I was filled up and strengthened all over again and ready to keep fighting the good fight. For that entire year and a half, SANE Church was my life, my faith grew stronger, and I kept obeying God's word.

A few months later, Pastor Dane started missing Bible study more often, sometimes even missing church on Sunday. None of us knew why, but we started gathering at each other's apartments to hold our own Bible studies and pray for him. We tried to focus on the Word as much as possible and to understand that it might just be temporary absences. But our pastor was not as consistently there as he had been. Other people would preach and teach the Word of God to us, but no one was as effective to my spirit as Pastor Dane had been. They didn't break the Word down the way he did. The messages were less relatable and did not penetrate my spirit the same way. Slowly but surely, we started hearing that he was making music again and was going back to try his hand in the entertainment industry. The news of him signing to a record label started by another popular rapper broke my heart into many pieces.

I was being distracted from the message by paying too much attention to the life of the messenger. Many people in the congregation were confused and slowly stopped attending church. We didn't understand the pastor's reasoning, but now, as a spiritually mature Christian, I see that it was not our place to find his reasons. During that season, many hearts were broken, and confusion spread over the city like weeds. The flock of strong and radical believers grew weak, and many of us gradually returned to our old habits. I slowly wearied of the things I was there for and what I had learned. Before I knew it, I was backsliding, drinking wine at home and crying, not caring about work or anything else. Men were starting to look more appealing to me, and the eyes that I had shut were open again. Soon afterward, I broke my celibacy. After 16 months of being faithful and on fire for God it was all over. The spiritual high was gone, and I didn't want to hear anything about God. I visited SANE again, but when Pastor Dane preached I didn't feel the power I had once felt, so I stopped going. It was almost as if his sermons were watered down to me, diluted by something else.

After it was confirmed that our beloved Pastor Dane Lewis had indeed returned to the music industry, and a music video was released, my heart hardened. Many of us staggered in our spirit and lost ourselves. It was like the head fell from a body and then some of the limbs fell apart and eventually disappeared.

I remember walking into a strip club one night to get a drink and seeing another member there. There was always a silent nod when I met someone in the world who I knew from the church. We were hurt, some of us were confused, but we just never spoke about it. As for me, I can tell you that I turned away from God, and it was like my ears went deaf. I felt like I had been dropped back into the wilderness of the world without warning. I had to survive without armor, and the only weapon I carried was the Word, which I did know and remained in my heart. Although, I could not use my weapon effectively, because I no longer believed in it. In that particular season of my life, I felt that if Pastor Dane didn't stand firm and believe his own teachings or the Word of God he had taught me, why should I?

I was so concerned about the things he was doing personally in his music career, that I was blinded. For years, I carried this pain in my heart, along with anger and doubt in the Word of God. I would often just ponder over questions like, why did he decide to go back to rapping in the secular industry? How does he think it could work, rapping and preaching? Did he go through a season of doubting God's word? Were we not good enough? Was it a lack of tithes and offerings? Did he make the decision for financial reasons?

These questions overwhelmed me, so I hardened my heart and moved on with my life. So many times I had to defend our ministry while I was a part of it, and now it was worse. The people who had never believed really made it hard for me. I was like a laughing stock and the situation was like a joke, and that got under my skin. No matter what had happened or what decisions he made, I still loved him as our pastor. We were like a family. No one enjoys people making fun of family members, so the subject became very sensitive to me, and I still wouldn't let anyone bad-mouth him in my presence! But God only knows how many nights I went home and wept alone. The thought that God was just a myth arose in my mind.

Today, I can look back and ask, "Why was I giving so much attention to Pastor Dane's personal life and career choices. What was I thinking? Why did I let his decisions detour my spiritual walk?" I could easily have gone to a different church if I wanted to and continued my walk, but I didn't. This was the crossroads where, I must admit I was not worshipping God. I was worshipping and idolizing my Pastor. As a babe in Christ, I didn't understand what was happening to me. Something deep in my soul knew that it was no way that he had been led by the enemy to mock the Word of God. That could not be possible to me. The entire ministry experienced too many spiritual occurrences that gave evidence that the Word was true in him and to him! I knew God spoke through him and I could not ever think otherwise for longer than a minute.

Chapter 6

Seven Spirits, Eight Years

My journey of rebellion against the Word of God took me many places. I broke my celibacy shortly after I walked away from the ministry. My oldest son, Jaden, was conceived in the next few months. Although Jaden was a gift given to me by God, I was not ready to be a mother. But his father and I did our best. Once more it was an extreme swing, from celibacy to pregnancy. I was not upset about being pregnant, though. I felt relief, like I finally had something to cling to again. It was a new life and a new experience.

My son was seven months old when I

became frustrated with single motherhood. His dad and I had split up, and I didn't have family in Atlanta. My parents came to get him, and he went to stay with them for a few months. Meanwhile, I quickly got back into the social scene, this time not caring at all. I felt like I had tried God and his Word just didn't work. I dated an athlete, who I grew very close to. He was married but separated from his wife. That was one of the biggest mistakes of my life. I should have just remained his friend. So many negative things came of that situation.

But I also fell in love with a new hobby: music. I discovered that I enjoyed going to the studio and making music. I liked rapping. Some friends gave me the name "MaryJane," which they thought fit me well. My brother Alex taught me the fundamentals and enlightened me on the history of rap. Rapping was always his passion, but acting was mine, so I thought that I could succeed in "acting like a rapper." Before I knew it, my alter ego, MaryJane, became a character of its own. I had fun channeling my inner bad girl and getting away from the reality of

Alexis Miller. MaryJane was a character I could hide inside completely. But it masked a pain in my heart. I was lost and confused, and rapping was a band aid. I got to talk bad about whatever I wanted, and people enjoyed it.

Atlanta's music industry got to know me as a socialite and rapper called MaryJane. Before long, every successful artist there had either met me or had heard of an up-and-coming female rapper named MaryJane. My brother and I were in so many different studios together, meeting artists and buying tracks, that it became a part of our normal work week. We dove head-first into music and recorded some very hot records.

The night life was a huge part of the entertainment industry, and networking at major events from Atlanta to Miami became my life for the next three years. One thing I did learn was that if you're trying to make it in the music industry as a female artist, you can attract them with your image but you need to fight for your respect. It was fun, stressful, and discouraging all at once.

Spending money on studio time and beats, networking, and parties took a toll on me. I began to feel drained, so I brought in other forces to keep me going. Drugs and alcohol were a normal thing in the studios and in the clubs. I started clinging to alcohol like it was my best friend. It was a stronghold I could not leave. I had to be under the influence to go out, even to record at times, because if I was ever sober, I wouldn't enjoy the things going on around me.

Social media became a big deal, so I would make YouTube videos with my brothers Chico and Alex to gain attention and followers. This was when I met the twin brothers who were doing A&R for a record label in Atlanta. My brother and I grew very close to them. I started dating one and gave up rapping just like that. I found love and I no longer wanted any part of the industry.

Our relationship was rocky. He was very serious and wanted me to change my ways and grow up overnight. He wanted to have more kids, but that wasn't a desire of mines. When I discovered I was pregnant, I went behind his back to have an abortion. That was another huge mistake, but I had no remorse or any other feelings about it. I was still mad at the world. After struggling with being a single mother once, I was not ready to try again. So I broke his heart. It hurt him to no end when he heard what I had done.

Our relationship was never the same, but we kept dealing with each other, and a year later I became pregnant again—this time with twin boys. God was making a point to me, and I understood it at once. I had thought I could take matters into my own hands, but I couldn't. I would still have two more children, but now it would be two at once. That was when I learned the lesson that we are powerless and God has all the control. I aborted one baby and got pregnant with two.

I gave birth to Keon and Deon in September of 2011, and I was utterly depressed. I was not ready to be a mom once again, and I still wanted to pursue my dreams. How would I do that now, with three children? Post-partum depression took over my life for a few months, and I was not myself. Ramer and his twin brother Ronnie agreed to help out so that I could take a break to regroup and get better. While the babies were away with their dad and uncle, I started reaching out to my entertainment industry connects again. I did not take care of myself and I was not trying to get better. The medication that I was prescribed for post-partum depression made me sleep a lot so I stopped taking it. Next thing, I would be bored at home, missing my twins and I got so tired of fighting with their dad to bring them back home that I just went left. That is when my passion for music came back because I was angry and in pain.

I don't know if I was just numb to the reality of having to raise three children alone or if I was just afraid of the change completely. Going from a socialite and rapper, flying on private jets, shopping, and partying, to motherhood of 3 boys was too drastic of a change to face for me. Either way, the drinking and the partying started all over. I still hadn't dealt with my issues with God yet, and I did not want to face any of it. I blamed

Pastor Dane for a long time for my life having turned around the way it did. For years I carried anger and pain toward him in my heart.

God gave me a wonderful spiritual mentor during the years I wasn't in church, one who was always praying for me but I never paid attention to her long enough to hear what she was saying. That confirms to me that no matter where we find ourselves, God will send people to us. But we have to be willing to listen to them. For every wrong decision I made, she was there to pray me through it. No matter where, no matter what time, she would have me in her spirit, and she always called. For that I am forever thankful to Prophetess Sheila Ashley.

All the same, I started filming trailers for reality shows in the midst of my madness, and other ideas were pitched to me. I had friends who were on a hit reality show in Atlanta that portrayed love, hip-hop, situations, and drama in the music industry.

While we were joking around about one

particular couple who were facing marital problems, I commented that I could help them out and test their love for them. Next thing I knew, I was invited to a cabin party and found out the married man we had been joking about was there. I guess my friends wanted to test me and see how I would respond. No surprise, though, MaryJane delivered pure entertainment. I pressed him and challenged him in a game of strip poker. He said his wife had given him a pass, so as the entertainer I naturally am—and knowing that we were being filmed—I gave the world a show to look at. Once again, MaryJane had gotten herself into a chaotic situation, but this time it was on national television.

After the reality show aired it was two of the highest-rated episodes the reality show ever aired, my popularity as a bad girl went through the roof. And my personal downward spiral plummeted even further. I remember drinking all the time and taking prescription meds just to hide what I really needed to deal with. Jaden was with my mom, my twins were with their father, and he refused to even let me visit them. That made it even worse. I was a complete train wreck and suffering from depression in a way that I would not wish on anyone.

One morning the sun came up while I was in the studio with a few of my rapper friends. I vividly remember looking out the window and thinking to myself, "How did I get here? How did I get so far from God's will for my life? Why was I wasting so much time dancing with the devil?"

My life had taken a turn for the worst and I was not holding on to no good thing. Everything seemed meaningless. I would write songs from pain and confusion. This thing had really done a number on me. The sins were worse than before and I had no remorse.

I felt like it was easier to do bad rather than to do good. Nightmares would wake me up at night, I can count the times I actually prayed during that time. I walked around feeling heavy all the time, always drained and needed rest but would not get the rest I needed. The enemy really had me running into a brick wall and running fast. No concept of purpose just moving and doing what I told myself was going to work. I had so many plans and always talking about ideas without putting any real action behind it. As far as my personal relationships, I was unable to love anyone because I was not loving myself.

It was always weird to me when a guy would find interest in me. I would brush it off and tell them I was not interested and they should not be interested either. Who says that to a man? Why as women do we allow the enemy to use us and abuse us the way we do? The answer to that is that we will never know who we are or know our full potential until we know who we are through Christ.

Now that I reflect on my past I often think that I was trapped in my own mind and did not want a way out. I decided to take one man serious during that time and the only way he was able to penetrate my spirit the way he did was because he met me where I was. He was also going through some personal issues so we began to lean on one another's shoulders and fell in love. For a moment it felt good to love again but once again. Two hurt people cannot help each other without the Lord. So ultimately that relationship ended and was never put back together again. Then there it goes again I am gone and carrying more baggage with me.

As humans we lean on one another for comfort, courage, and love. Nothing is easy and some comfort zones are only comfortable for a limited time only. When Jesus is not in it that same situation can turn chaotic very fast. Those are the situations that we watch on television. The shows that reminds us that emotions can surely take over if we allow the enemy to tamper with our feelings and our minds. I can tell you today I want everlasting love and everlasting comfort. If he does not have God, I do not want him. Two people that love God may also have personal struggles, but two people that don't love God will just have hell here on earth.

I was not whole with myself so therefore I could not be whole with anyone else. These were the moments I would feel like I was self-destructing and in a sense that is exactly what I was doing. My attitude had changed, I was very bitter to my family and friends. I did not care about anyone's personal feelings at all. It was like something foreign was operating my body. It was such a dark place to be in that when I think back to it, I can still see the dark clouds that were over me. What had happened to me?

Luke 11:24-26

24When an unclean spirit goes out of a person, it passes through waterless places looking for rest but not finding any. Then it says, 'I will return to the home I left.' When it returns, it finds the house swept clean and put in order. 26Then it goes and brings seven other spirits more evil than itself, and they go in and live there, so the last state of that person is worse than the first."

Chapter 7

He Searches for His Sheep

This period of my life I call "Searching for His Sheep." I had taken a lot of wrong turns by this point. I turned so far away from God that it finally forced me to admit I needed him. I needed his Word and his spirit in my life again. I had witnessed his awakening once, and I yearned for it again.

I slowly weaned myself off alcohol, partying, and the night life. More and more often, I found myself looking for signs and trying to hear God's voice again. I would open my Bible, but it didn't speak to me like it once had, or maybe I didn't hear what it was saying. My ears were clogged, and my heart grew weary. I contemplated suicide at one point because I just wanted to give up. The enemy had nearly won the battle for my life, and I almost let him.

Then suddenly I started hearing a Word, but it wasn't the Word that I knew. My ears started to listen to words from the Koran. So I became interested in the Muslim religion, because it was the only thing I could hear. I didn't share my curiosity with anyone, but I did a lot of my own research and I compared stories from both books. The enemy was very cunning, playing on my pain as a Christian to try to convert me to Islam.

During my research, I traveled to Dubai. It was already one of my dream destinations, so when the opportunity arose I went. That never stopped me I was always a brave person, even as a kid. I shouldn't wait on anyone for things that I want to learn or discover for myself. So therefore I traveled 14 hours on a plane to Dubai Alone. When I arrived I was a little nervous not knowing what to expect. I used my common sense and judgement. I read the signs in the airport, asked questions, and slowly found comfort in knowing that I would be ok. I asked for assistance and I blended in with the locals. After getting into a cab to my hotel, I arrived and the hotel was very nice. Dubai itself was beautiful and I had never seen any place like it. The buildings' architecture and designs were amazing. I stayed in Dubai an entire week shopping in the city, taking city tours, getting my hair done at the local salon, & getting massage treatments at the spa. I dined alone and tried different dishes. I read different books and I learned so much about the culture there. I was on a journey in search of the truth. I wanted to learn about these people's religion and society.

I admired the way Muslim women covered their heads and bodies to respect their husbands and their religion. I wondered why Christian women didn't do the same—it seemed so honorable and upstanding. I bought a hijab and wore it out into the city. I enjoyed the way it felt to be covered.

I found myself sitting on Jumeirah Beach saying, "God why am I here? I know that Jesus is real, and no one has been able to teach me otherwise." Then I felt a peace come over me, and I knew I had tapped into my spirit again because that familiar feeling of chills ran up my spine again. The wind blew softly against my face, and then it was like a movie played in my mind. I realized at that moment it wasn't Pastor Dane's fault that I had turned away from God. It was my spiritual immaturity. That had led me to esteem my pastor above God, and that wasn't right. I realized that God gives us apostles, prophets, evangelists, pastors, and teachers. He never said that he gave us perfect people. Our leaders are used by God to teach his word, clarify his messages, and edify the body of Christ. But they still have their own lives outside the church, their own struggles, families, and personal obstacles. We should never hold them in such high regard that they can't make mistakes. They are human beings, at the end of the day, who have been called to carry out an assignment.

I thank God for my visit to Dubai, because

on Jumeirah Beach that day I was enlightened like never before. We should love and respect our spiritual leaders, but we should stay focused on the messages they teach us.

My last day there I did not leave my hotel room much. I stayed in the room reading the word. My flight was leaving that evening so I went down to the restaurant to have dinner. It was at that restaurant that I would meet a very nice Arab man that offered to pay for my meal and invited himself to my table. He insisted that I visit his country again soon so that he would have time to show me around and take me to the mosque in Abu Dhabi. We exchanged information so we could keep in touch. One month later I went back to Dubai, this time I traveled to Abu Dhabi, so I could experience the traditional side and the mosque. I really enjoyed how he treated me like a princess. He always dropped me off at the door of my hotel after a day of sightseeing.

Two days before the Abu Dhabi trip was over he said he would introduce me to someone that could give me more information about the religion than he could. I had already changed my mind about wanting to convert to Islam but I still met him and asked a few questions for clarity. He was unable to give me any new information that would pose any other questions in my mind about Jesus Christ being the only begotten son. At that point I felt like God had covered me and gave me the wisdom I was searching for in that country.

I traveled back to Atlanta and began to pray, spend time in my Word, and meditate as I had before. The difference was that I had been through so much that I appreciated the presence of the Lord more and was balanced in understanding it all.

Two months later, I attended a Christmas event held by a friend who was a successful business owner in Atlanta. The party was very high profile, and many celebrities were in attendance. It was sponsored by Hublot, a watch manufacturer known for its expensive timepieces. That night I didn't have even one glass of champagne. It was strange, but I was feeling at peace and just wanted to enjoy the event. Eventually, the host took to the microphone to say they were having a Christmas giveaway for one lucky lady: a Hublot watch. We just had to put our names in a box on the front table. God whispered in my heart, "It is yours," right before I wrote my name.

I saw many other young ladies cheating and writing their names more than once. What no one at the party knew was that I had a story about a designer watch that was given to me nine years before that night. When I was saved at SANE Church, I sowed a seed to a young woman on our praise team. It was a Michele watch worth about $1000.00. I released it from my life because it kept my heart tied to the person who had given it to me, and I was trying to get over that relationship. After that I never wore another watch and never wanted anyone to buy me one. I did always say, though, that I wanted a special watch one day, which I knew God would give me.

Butterflies were in my stomach as the host

of the party, also a famous rapper, took the mic and pulled a piece of paper out of the box. He looked up and said, "The winner of the Hublot watch is Alexis Miller." I smiled and looked around as I walked up to receive this wonderful gift worth $10,000.00.

This was such a defining experience to reassure me that my life was re-aligning itself with where it should be. *Wow!* I had actually reaped what I sowed from nine years earlier, and it was a much better return. I found myself going deeper and deeper in the word at home and spending more time in prayer. That was the moment I needed. It also made me feel like I had sown into good ground.

Luke 15:4

What man of you having and hundred sheep, if he lose one of them, doth not leave the ninety and nine in the wilderness, and go after that which is lost?

Ezekiel 34:12

As a shepherd seeketh out his flock in the day that he is among his sheep that are scattered; so will I seek out my sheep, and will deliver them out of all places where they have been scattered in the cloudy and dark day.

Chapter 8

Redeemed and Restored

This chapter begins with the understanding that God has a purpose for all our lives. We will not know or be ready to hear his instructions without the Bible, the church, and a personal relationship with him. We also must be comfortable enough to repent when we are wrong and to go to him in prayer. We cannot do this all alone. We all need God, and we need to listen to the Holy Spirit in our hearts. We must align ourselves so that we are in a position to receive his blessings. If we cannot hear him, we cannot do what he needs us to do.

We all need a church where we can

fellowship and worship with other believers. A place where we can draw closer to God in our personal relationships and adore people like he adores us. The church should be a place to find comfort, a place where we are uplifted and share intimate moments with other believers. My journey back to God's side has been rewarding but still challenging. It was hard to find the desire in my heart to attend just any church. I prayed and asked God to send me to a place where I can receive the Word and get right back on task as if I had never left. The Lord led me to a small church that I instantly fell in love with. The pastor was amazing at breaking the Word of God down for us. I officially rededicated and was also baptized there. I did not join that particular church but my entire time there was very inspiring. My mentor advised me that this particular pastor was used as a catalyst to get me back on track.

Sometimes when I look back, I still cry when I reflect on my past and the foolishness that God carried me through. The tears are tears of joy and gratitude in my heart for the fact that God covered me with so much grace and mercy. His love is unconditional, and for that I must serve him and let him use my gifts for his purposes. The spiritual connections that I have gained along the way has been incredible and long lasting. These bonds with the special people that have stuck around through my good times and my bad times have shown me true love. I am grateful to them for it. Because I know many times a broken person is a hard person to love.

Throughout these past years I know I have hurt people, disappointed people, and also have gotten hurt myself. I am on a mission to ask for forgiveness and also to forgive so that God can heal and recover any and every relationship that may need to be recovered. I do understand that some friendships may never be restored and those are the ones that I can have a peace about because that means the no matter what the purpose was, it was fulfilled.

I am so honored and thankful that you were interested enough in me or my story that you have read this memoir. For that I say thank you and the love you have shown has melted my heart. I would have never thought that all the mess I had been through would one day became a message.

To any young woman reading this that have made similar mistakes or other mistakes. Please forgive yourself and do not live in condemnation. God forgives us, we can go on and start a new life with Christ with a renewed mind and a renewed spirit. Dedicate your life to the lord and try God he will never fail you nor forsake you. Unlike these men, that we have dated in the past. Our God will not stand us up, he will show up for the date and he will be on time.

I am deeply thankful to my pastors, my spiritual mentors, and every leader in ministry who has touched my life. In one way or in many ways; the ones who fed my spirit in my past and the ones who are in my present. We need them to help us take this awesome journey that God has placed all of his sons and daughters on. God loves us, so he gave us his only begotten son. In the name of Jesus, AMEN.

Jesus, What A Wonder You Are.

Psalm 147:3
He healeth the broken in heart and bindeth up their wounds.

Ephesians 4:22-24
That ye put off concerning the former conversation the old man, which is corrupt according to the deceitful lusts; 23And be renewed in the spirit of your mind; 24And that ye put on the new man, which after God is created in righteousness and true holiness.

About The Author

Alexis Miller is a mother 3 boys, 4yr old twins and a 9yr old. She is 32yrs old and currently lives in Atlanta. Alexis was born Sunset, La. She has always had a passion for acting since age 6. Alexis was crowned Hal Jackson's Talented Teen 1998- 99. From that experience she traveled abroad and landed an acting contract with an award winning talent agency in Hollywood, CA. After graduating high school, she decided to move to Atlanta where she began her life as an adult. She has always been a socialite and is known by many movers and shakers in the entertainment industry from California to Atlanta, GA.

During her early years in Atlanta she quickly grasped a love for God and found an intimate relationship with Jesus Christ. Alexis was saved at 20 years old and fell in love with the word and her church SANE Church Int'l. The 2 years there was so awakening to her spirit. She experienced some changes that were being made in the ministry and she drifted away from God. At that moment, Alexis decided to embark on a music career as her alter ego "MaryJane." Her life went through many obstacles twists and turns down the wrong path and this is where her story uplifts inspires, and will touch many. She made a few very controversial guest appearances on VH1's hit reality TV show "Love and Hip Hop Atlanta.

Her experience as an artist/Tv personality has cultivated her entire testimony. The objective to this memoir is to share her testimony. This book was written in hopes of bringing believers back to the church. Especially those that have left for various reasons. She hopes we can regain focus on how important it is to belong to a church and fellowship with other believers. No matter what our leaders in ministry may go through she emphasizes the Power of Prayer that we must have for them. Teaching the Word is not easy, so we must show our leaders love and dedication so that they always are built up and able to deliver God's messages and clarify his visions.

Alexis's passion for God and the church comes from her own mistakes in early years as a young believer. She goes in detail in this memoir and admits she was paying too much attention to what the messenger was doing and got distracted from the message. This is an important time for The Body of Christ and we must remain steadfast on the Word. God has given us apostles, prophets, evangelists, pastors, and teachers. He never said he was giving us Perfect People. {"If you have been church hurt or left church because of any type of ministry confusion. I stand with you my brothers and sisters and I say let's rebuild and recover together."} We all need a church to call home, a place of refuge, to hear God's messages. It's time to get "Church Healed."

Acknowledgments

Suzzana & Madilla Hurks
Leona & Francis Singleton Sr.
Linda & Winnie Jason
Charles & Terryon Miller
Alexander Miller
Angela & Samantha Lee
Willie Singleton-Guillory
Brittany Singleton
Rev. Solomen
Robert & Shirley Dupre
Betty Mitchell
Cheryl Monroe
Dee Hartman
Geri Malveaux
Jane Harley
Hal Jackson's Foundation
Adele Dantzler
Mrs. Lennie & Mr. Robert
Gracy Warren
Timell Patterson
Jimmy JD Davis
Lyn Brown
Juandolyn Stringer
Kendall Hallman
Bishop Clarence E. McClendon
Pastor Craig & Lady Oliver, & EBC Family, Atlanta, GA
Pastor Sheila & James Ashley, & Total Agape Atlanta
Zion Travelers Baptist Church, Sunset, LA
El Elyon Ministries, Atlanta, GA
Spirit of Faith Ministries, Smyrna, GA
Pastor Derrick & Lady Flanagan, Christ Abundant Life